The Story of the Wright Brothers

Bruce LaFontaine

DOVER PUBLICATIONS, INC.
Mineola, New York

Bibliographical Note

The Story of the Wright Brothers is a new work, first published by Dover Publications, Inc., in 2000.

International Standard Book Number
ISBN-13: 978-0-486-41321-1
ISBN-10: 0-486-41321-7

Manufactured in the United States by LSC Communications
41321708   2017
www.doverpublications.com

INTRODUCTION

The idea of flight has always stirred people's imaginations. Myths and tales of mankind imitating the flight of the birds date back to ancient times. During the Renaissance, Leonardo Da Vinci applied his genius to the problem of flight and made numerous detailed drawings of flying machines. But it was not until the late 19th century that serious study of and experimentation in powered flight began.

Two paths of research eventually converged into the Wright brothers' first successful piloted, powered, controlled flight by a heavier-than-air craft in 1903. The first was taken by theorists who studied the physiology and movement of birds. This led to the design and construction of unpowered gliders that utilized the elements affecting flight—*lift* (the air force that provides upward motion); *thrust* (the air force exerted to give forward motion); *drag* (the retarding air force opposing thrust); and *gravity* (the pull of Earth's mass on the plane). Aviation pioneers such as Sir George Cayley, Otto Lilienthal, and Octave Chanute made great contributions in the area of flight theory.

The other path was taken by engineers and mechanics who worked to develop *power plants*—engines producing thrust force—to propel early aircraft prototypes. American inventor Samuel P. Langley and the Wright brothers represent this avenue of research. Initially, steam engines were used to power experimental flying machines, but the excessive weight and relatively low power of the steam engine proved unsuccessful. Not until the development of the internal combustion engine in the second half of the 19th century was a lightweight yet powerful propulsion mechanism available. Until 1939, when the use of turbojets proved feasible, airplanes used a piston engine similar to an automobile's.

The Wright brothers combined the knowledge gleaned from these two paths of research with their own keen mechanical inventiveness. When Milton Wright brought his young sons a toy helicopter—its twin propellers set in motion by twisting a rubber band—he could never have imagined the momentous events that the simple plaything foreshadowed.

Wilbur Wright was born on a farm in Indiana in 1867, Orville in Dayton, Ohio, in 1871. Their early projects included Orville's home-built printing press and publishing business, and the brothers' profitable bicycle shop in Dayton, which provided funds to finance their experiments. The two developed a close bond; Wilbur wrote that it seemed as though he and his brother "thought together." Certainly, their joint efforts formed a cornerstone of aviation history.

They began their aeronautic experiments in 1899 using biplane kites; by 1900 they were flying tethered kite-style gliders. The brothers worked for three years, conducting hundreds of test flights and gaining valuable flight data. By 1903, they were ready to test their *Flyer*, powered by a 4-cylinder internal combustion engine designed and built by the Wrights and their mechanic, Charles Taylor. On December 17th, with Orville as the pilot, the *Flyer* took off, flew for 12 seconds, and gently touched back down, achieving the first sustained powered, piloted flight. The era of the airplane had begun!

The story of the Wright brothers is a tale of experimentation, persistence, and courage. Risking their lives, they repeatedly launched test flights, analyzed the results, and made modifications. From 1903 to 1912, the Wright brothers built and flew a succession of more advanced aircraft. They demonstrated their flying machines in the United States and Europe, achieving widespread fame while providing inspiration for other early aviation pioneers. Sadly, in 1912, Wilbur died from typhoid fever at the age of 45. Dayton, Ohio, observed the death of this outstanding citizen with three minutes of silence; even the phone service was halted. Orville lived on to age 77, witnessing the transformation of the world brought about by the brothers' historic invention. Together, they took the idea of flight from the realm of imagination into the world of reality, flying into the history books on the wings of their mechanical genius, hard work, and daring spirit.

1. Sir George Cayley's Glider, 1849. An early pioneer of flight was Englishman Sir George Cayley (1773–1857). Beginning in 1804, he built small flying models of gliders, followed by larger "kite"-style gliders controlled by a line from the ground. Cayley described the basic principles of flight in his 1810 book, *On Aerial Navigation.* By 1849, Cayley had begun building full-scale flying gliders such as this one, which carried a 60-lb. boy over a short distance. The glider featured a boat-shaped fuselage, tri-level wings, a pilot seat, tail assembly, and side-mounted oarlike "flappers," intended to increase flight propulsion. Sir George Cayley's experiments and test flights were crucial to other early aviation pioneers.

2. Félix du Temple's Steam-Powered Aircraft, 1874. Around 1858, French naval officer Félix du Temple began building and flying small model gliders powered by a clockwork spring mechanism, later moving on to models powered by lightweight miniature steam engines. The Frenchman then built a full-scale steam-powered aircraft capable of carrying a pilot. The machine shown above, flown in 1874, was launched from an inclined "ski-jump"-type ramp; it flew only in short "hops" because its lifting power was not great enough for flight. Steam-powered aircraft were a dead end; the lighter, more powerful internal combustion engine would lead to true powered, controlled flight.

3. Otto Lilienthal's Glider, 1891. One of the most influential early pioneers of flight was German-born Otto Lilienthal (1848–1896). He designed and flew numerous gliders, beginning in 1891. His work was critical in developing the curved or "cambered" airfoil wing necessary to create the "lift" needed for flight. In the aircraft shown, the pilot was suspended between the wings—shifting his weight created some degree of controlled directional movement. In 1894 Lilienthal constructed in Berlin a hill, shown above, for his glider flight studies. From this and other perches, Lilienthal made over 2,000 test flights, ranging from 150 to 1,500 feet. This pioneering aviator was killed in a crash landing in 1896.

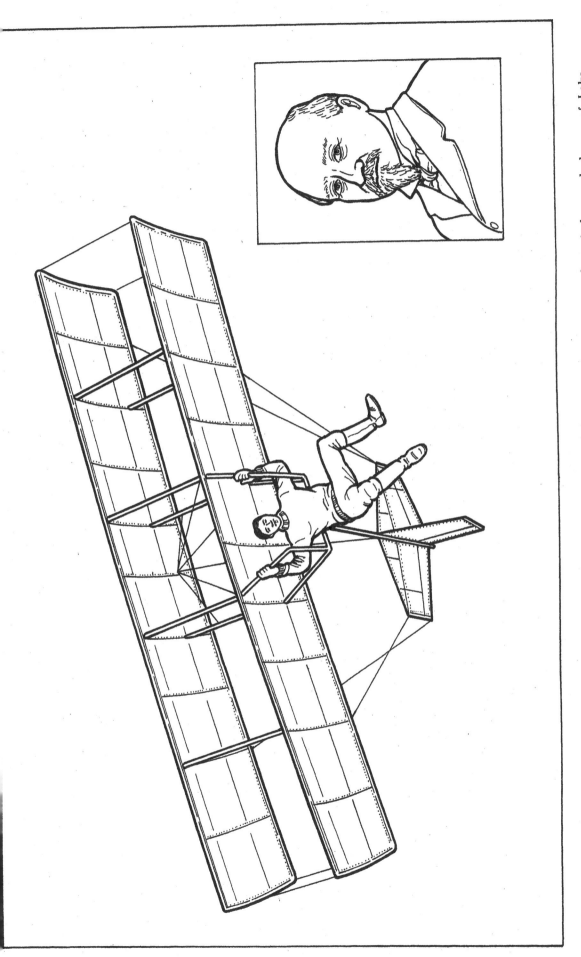

4. Octave Chanute's Glider Experiments. Another early aviation researcher who influenced the Wright brothers' work was Octave Chanute (1832–1910). Chanute had a successful career as a civil engineer before becoming involved with glider design, construction, and test flights. In 1894 he published a book on aerodynamics, *Progress in Flying Machines.* By 1896, he was conducting glider demonstration flights on the windy sand dunes of Lake Michigan. Along with assistant Augustus Herring, Chanute designed and tested numerous gliders. Limited directional control was accomplished by the pilot's shifting his weight. Chanute's work helped establish the necessary control and stabilization techniques used in the Wright Flyers.

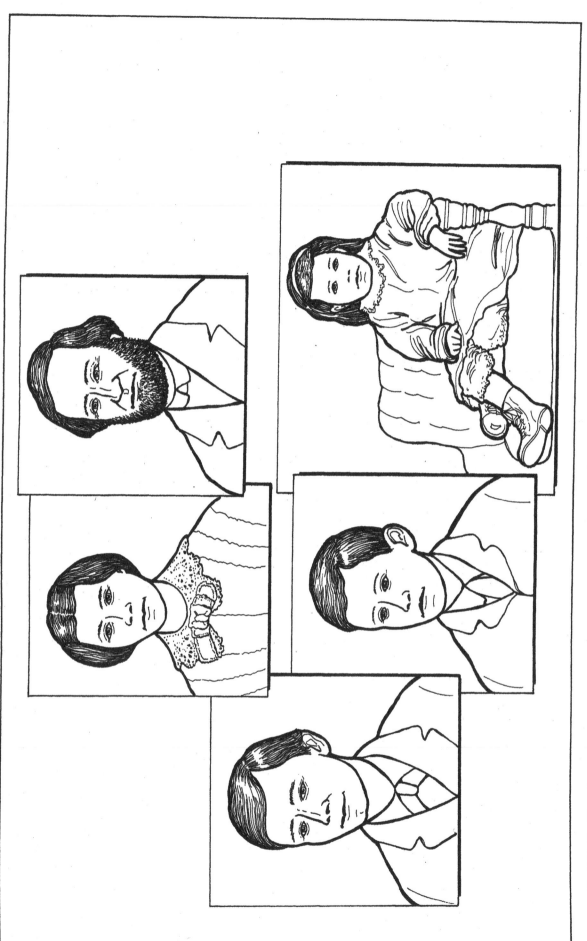

5. Wright Family Portraits, 1878. (Top right) Milton Wright, Wilbur and Orville's father (1828–1917), was an itinerant clergyman who became a bishop of the United Brethren Protestant Church. (Top left) Susan Koerner Wright, their mother (1831–1889), attended Hartsville College, Indiana, and was known (Lower left) Wilbur Wright (1867–1912). (Lower middle) Orville Wright (1871–1948). (Lower right) Katharine Wright, their sister (1874–1929), committed much time and energy to her brothers' pursuit of their goals. Brothers Reuchlin and Lorin, whose lives developed in distinctly different directions from Wilbur's and

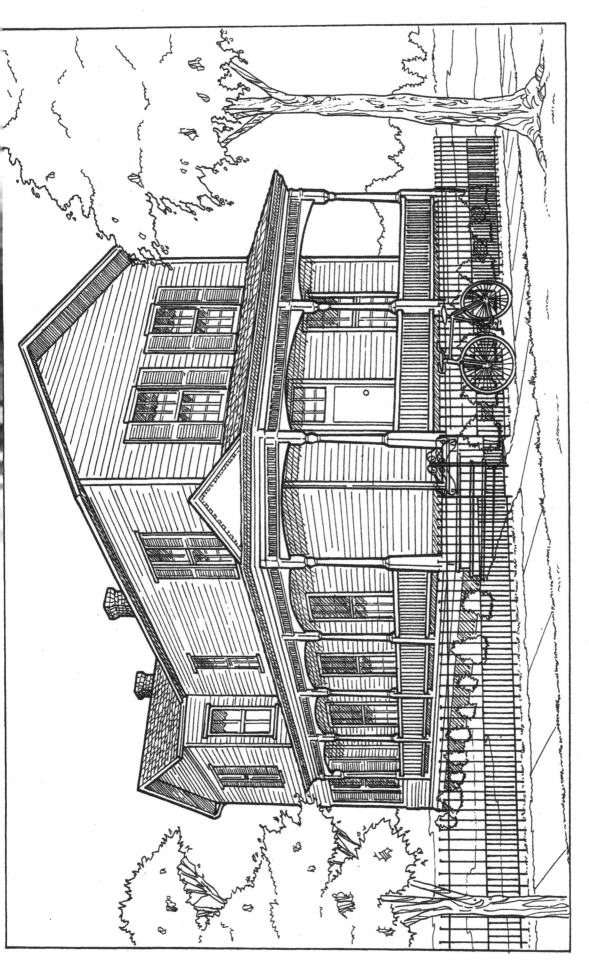

6. Wright Brothers Boyhood Home, Dayton, Ohio. The Wright family lived in this 2-story frame house at No. 7 Hawthorn Street in Dayton, Ohio, from 1871 to 1878, and again from 1885 to 1914. As a traveling clergyman, Bishop Milton Wright moved the family to Cedar Rapids, Iowa, and Richmond, Virginia, before returning to Hawthorn Street. The house (along with the brothers' bicycle shop) was moved piece by piece in 1936 to Dearborn, Michigan, to become part of Henry Ford's Greenfield Village. It was here that automobile manufacturer Henry Ford moved selected factories and houses to reconstruct the way of life of pre-World War I America.

7. Wright Brothers Bicycle Shop, Dayton, Ohio. In 1892, Wilbur and Orville began operating a bicycle repair shop in Dayton. By 1896, they were building bicycles of their own design at the shop shown above, located at 1127 West 3rd Street in Dayton. Both brothers were gifted mechanically and became expert machinists, acquiring the skills needed to fabricate parts for their gliders and powered aircraft. In their cycle shop, the Wrights built the first wind tunnel machine, which they used to evaluate airfoil wing shapes for their aircraft.

8. Wright Brothers First Kite-Style Glider, 1900. The Wright brothers began their experiments with flying machines by building a winged glider (shown here) controlled from the ground by lines attached to the wing and forward horizontal elevator. The Wrights found a location suitable for a test site at the Kill Devil Hills sand dunes near Kitty Hawk, North Carolina. In 1900, the brothers set up a tent camp and began testing their machine. This first glider had a horizontal elevator and wings joined by vertical struts. The wings were constructed from wooden ribs (spars) that were covered with cloth and coated with a paintlike substance to stiffen the cloth.

9. Wright Brothers Shed Camp, Kitty Hawk, North Carolina, 1901. By 1901 Wilbur and Orville had built a more substantial and comfortable temporary residence at the Kill Devil Hills testing site. The brothers conducted further flight tests, first with gliders, then kitchen, where Orville did the cooking, and sleeping quarters. The Wrights soon learned to conduct their experiments in late summer, fall, and early winter—during midsummer, mosquitoes and sand fleas made for miserable living conditions on the dunes.

10. Wright Brothers Glider No. 2, 1901. The Wright brothers continued their research at Kill Devil Hills with the 1901 test flight of their Glider No. 2. This aircraft had a larger wing-lifting area than their first glider, and was also equipped with a more substantial forward elevator. The improved control system allowed for lateral (turning) movement by "wing warping"—twisting the wing using control cables to induce a gentle banked turn. The front-mounted horizontal elevator changed the glider's nose-up and nose-down positions. With Glider No. 2, the brothers had devised a machine with better stability and control—critical elements of their goal of developing a powered flying machine.

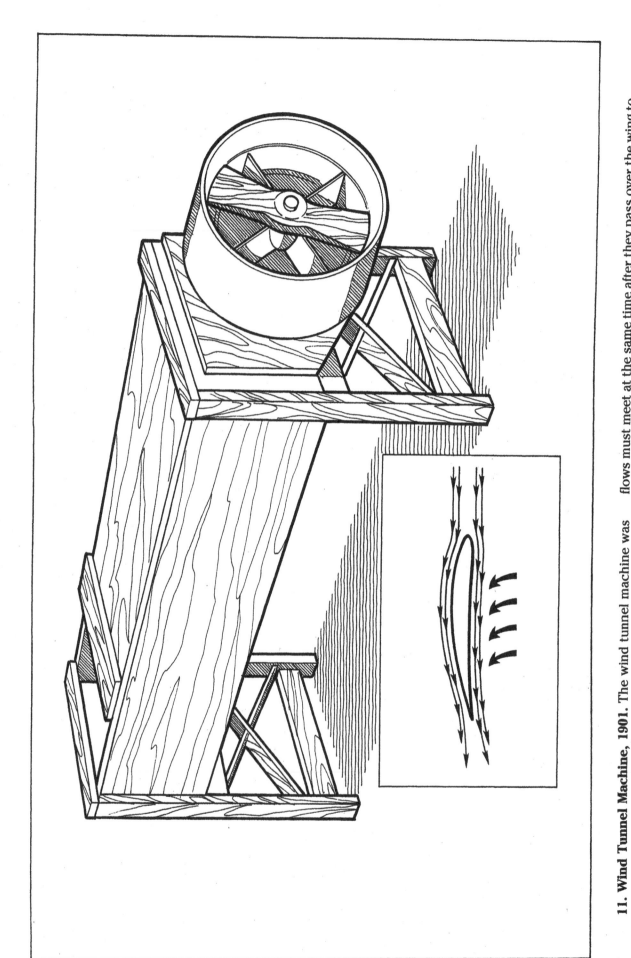

11. Wind Tunnel Machine, 1901. The wind tunnel machine was designed and built by the Wright brothers in 1901 at their Dayton, Ohio, bike shop. They used it to develop the "airfoil" wing shape needed to provide lifting power for flight. An airfoil wing is curved ("cambered") along the top and bottom; the curve on the top sur-

flows must meet at the same time after they pass over the wing to avoid forming a vacuum, so the air flows faster over the curved top surface. The faster air flows, the less pressure it creates, so the pressure on the top of the wing is less than the pressure on the underside. The greater pressure from the underside causes lift.

12. First Piloted Flights of Glider No. 2, 1902. The Wright brothers returned to Kill Devil Hills in August, 1902, to continue their glider tests. They built a new glider with twin rudders in preparation for a piloted flight. The wingspan was increased to 35 feet, creating 305 square feet of wing area. The front elevator was 15 square feet in area, while the rear rudder was 12 square feet. On September 19, flights began, with Wilbur and Orville alternating as pilot. Dozens of test glides were made from September 1902 through early 1903. Information gained from these glider tests was incorporated into the design of the brothers' next machine, the historic engine-powered Wright *Flyer I*.

13. Side View of Wright *Flyer I*
Length (nose to tail): 21 ft. 1 in.
Distance between top and bottom wing: 5 ft.
Total weight: 605 lbs.

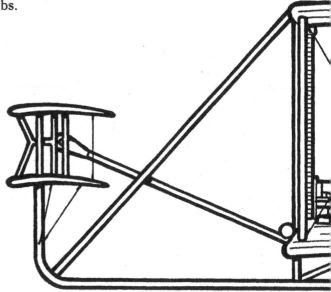

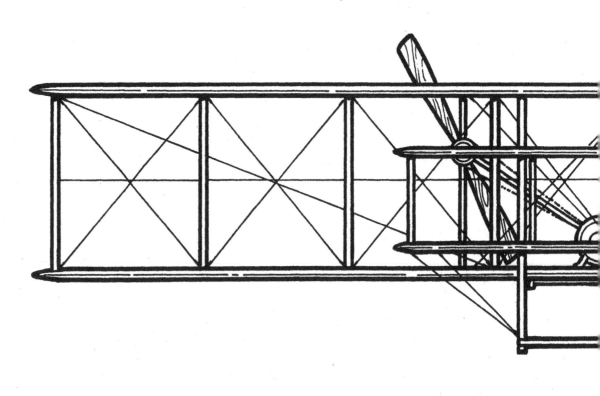

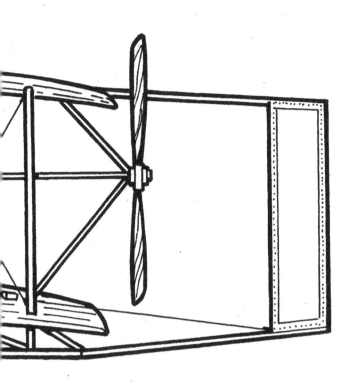

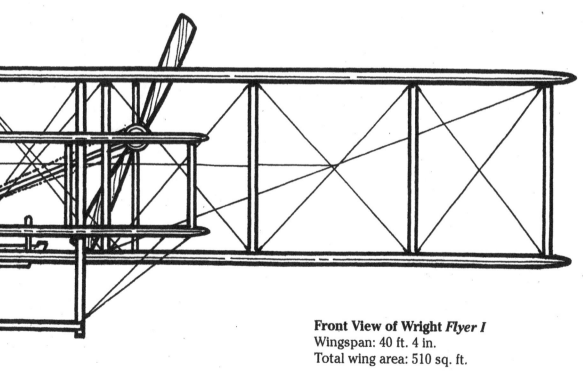

Front View of Wright *Flyer I*
Wingspan: 40 ft. 4 in.
Total wing area: 510 sq. ft.

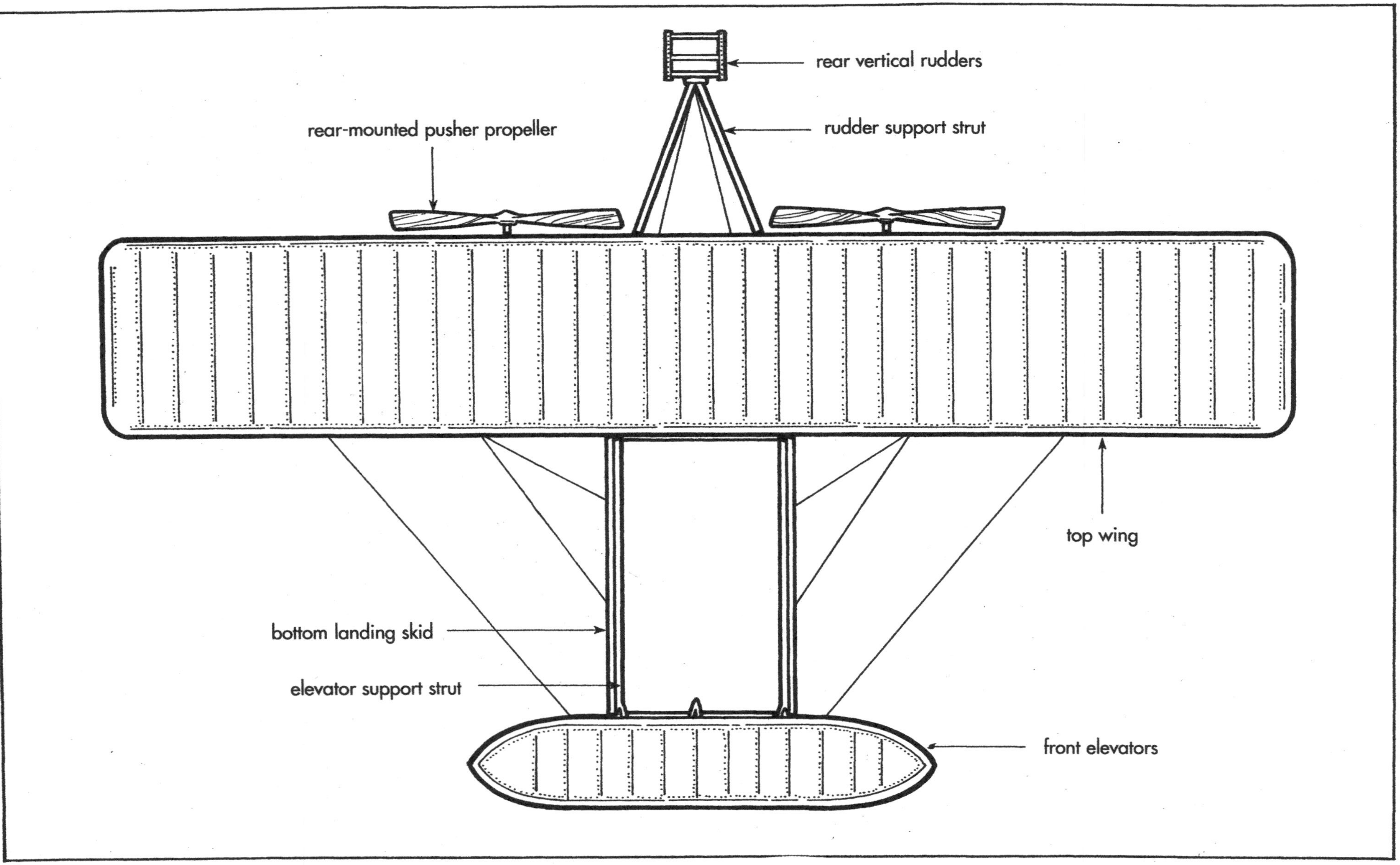

rear vertical rudders

rudder support strut

rear-mounted pusher propeller

top wing

front elevators

bottom landing skid

elevator support strut

14. Top View of Wright *Flyer I*

15. Wilbur with Wright *Flyer I*, 1903. In September 1903, the Wright brothers returned to Kitty Hawk to begin assembly of their first powered aircraft, the *Flyer I*. The biplane had a 4-cylinder internal combustion engine designed and built by the brothers and their mechanic, Charles Taylor. The pilot would lie on his stomach in a harness connected to the wings by control cables. He could move his hips to adjust the wing warping for directional control. He had a hand lever to change the up-and-down pitch of the front elevators. The 12-horsepower engine turned a pair of chain-driven propellers. The "landing gear" was a pair of sledlike skids.

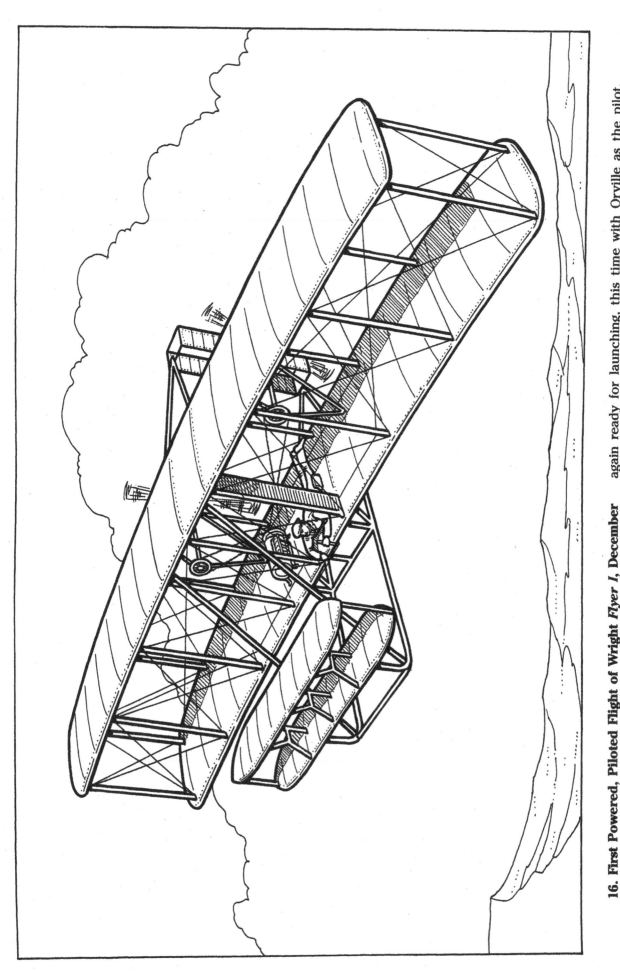

16. First Powered, Piloted Flight of Wright _Flyer 1_, December 17, 1903. By December 14, 1903, the _Flyer 1_ was ready for its first test flight; Wilbur was the pilot. It was launched from a 60-foot-long monorail track. The first attempt at takeoff failed, causing slight damage to the spindly craft. Repairs took until December 17. At 10:35 on the morning of December 17, 1903, the _Flyer_ was again ready for launching, this time with Orville as the pilot. Moving into a 20-mph headwind, the _Flyer_ lifted into the air and flew under its own power for 12 seconds, over a distance of over 100 feet. Three more flights were made that day, with Wilbur piloting the final flight over a distance of 852 feet in 59 seconds. From this modest start, the era of powered, controlled flight had begun!

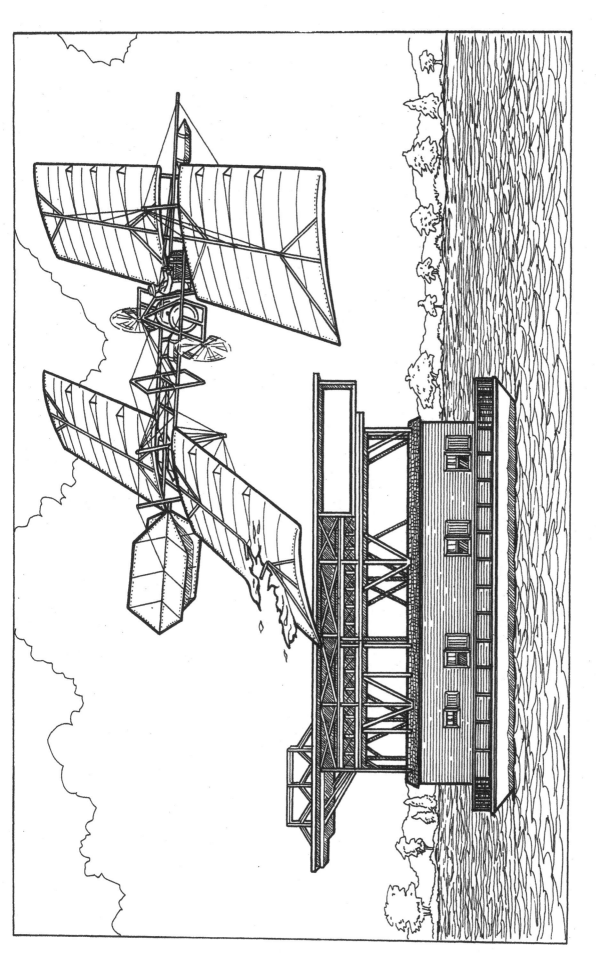

17. Samuel P. Langley's "Aerodrome," 1903. Samuel Pierpont Langley (1834-1906) had a distinguished career as secretary of the Smithsonian Institution before beginning his flight studies around the age of 50. Langley built his first "Aerodrome" model in 1891; in 1896, Aerodrome No. 5, launched from a catapult, stayed aloft for 90 seconds, becoming the first heavier-than-air powered machine to fly. In 1903, Langley tested a full-sized, powered, piloted Aerodrome; unfortunately, a wing snagged as the craft was catapulted off the ramp, and the Aerodrome tumbled into the Potomac River. In 1914, aviator and exhibition flyer Glenn Curtiss modified, rebuilt, and successfully flew the Langley Aerodrome over Keuka Lake, near Hammondsport, New York.

18. Thérèse Peltier, First Woman to Fly, 1908. During this period, European inventors were also at work on flying machines, spurred on by the Wright brothers' achievements. By 1908, a number of aircraft were being flown by these pioneering aviators. On July 8, 1908, in Turin, Italy, aviation history was made when French sculptor Thérèse Peltier became the first woman passenger to fly in a heavier-than-air craft. She was taken aloft by her friend Léon Delagrange for a 650-foot flight. Peltier also made several solo flights; by 1910, several American and European women had become pilots.

19. Wilbur Wright at Controls of _Flyer_ in France, 1908.
From 1904 to 1905, the Wright brothers built and flew two new aircraft, the _Flyer II_ and the _Flyer III_. These machines had stronger components, a more powerful engine, and an upright seating position for the pilot in the _Flyer III_. By May 1905, the _Flyer III_ had made a 20-mile, 33-minute flight at 35 mph. The Wrights demonstrated their aircraft for both private companies and government officials, hoping for contracts to build more planes. Initially, the U.S. government showed only modest interest; European countries, however, were greatly interested in the brothers' flying machines. During 1908 and 1909, Wilbur and Orville successfully demonstrated their airplane in European countries, including France, Germany, and Spain.

20. Louis Blériot Flies the English Channel, 1909. The most famous European aviator of this era was Frenchman Louis Blériot. He flew into the aviation history books with his daring solo flight over the English Channel in a frail single-wing airplane of his own design. His type XI monoplane was powered by a 3-cylinder, 25-hp engine. On July 25, 1909, Blériot flew from Calais, France, to Dover, England, a distance of 24 miles over the open sea. For this first aerial crossing of the Channel, Blériot was hailed as a national hero in France.

21. Wilbur Wright and King Alfonso XIII, 1909. During their 1909 demonstration tour of Europe, Wilbur and Orville met with many royal heads of state. The European monarchs showed great interest in the remarkable new flying machine of the inventive Americans. Wilbur is shown here with King Alfonso XIII of Spain discussing the control system of the Wright *Flyer III* at Pau, near the Pyrenees mountains in southwest France.

22. Orville Wright and Crown Prince Friedrich Wilhelm, 1909. Orville demonstrated the Wright *Flyer III* in Germany in 1909, breaking his own record for two-man flight on September 18 with a time of 1 hour and 35 minutes. Orville is shown here with Crown Prince Friedrich Wilhelm at Tempelhof Field, near Berlin. The prince was greatly interested in flying and accompanied Orville briefly on October 2, 1909, becoming the first member of European royalty to experience a flight in a powered aircraft.

23. Wilbur and Orville Wright, 1910. These portraits show brothers Wilbur (left, and in inset picture) and Orville (right, and in inset picture) on the front porch of the Hawthorn Street house in Dayton, Ohio, in 1910; Wilbur is 43, Orville 39.

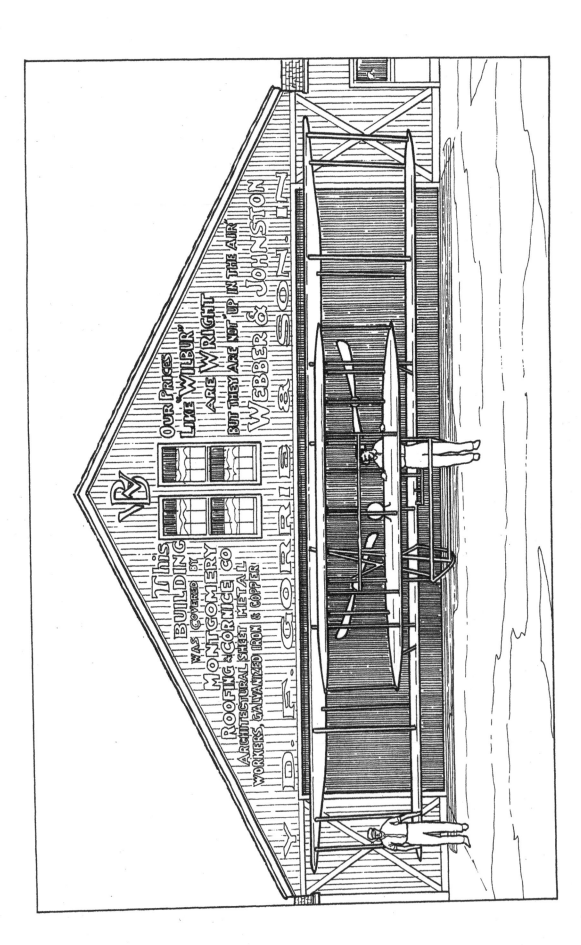

24. Wright Company Flying School, 1910. As a result of their aviation success and the public's interest in flight, the Wright brothers began temporary operation of a flying school in Montgomery, Alabama. The location was selected for its mild weather, conducive to year-round flight instruction. Orville was the chief instructor for the first student, childhood friend Walter Brookins. The school was moved to an airfield near Dayton soon after. One of the students' tasks was to chase cows from the field before flights. Here, students are shown preparing a *Flyer III* for takeoff.

25. Glenn Curtiss's Model E Flying Boat, 1912. Glenn H. Curtiss, the Wright brothers' chief American competitor, was born in 1878 in Hammondsport, upstate New York. A gifted mechanic, Curtiss turned to airplane development when he became involved with the Aerial Experiment Association, co-founded by Alexander Graham Bell. By 1911, Curtiss was building airplanes powered by his own V-8 engines. He then began conducting experiments with water-launched aircraft at his Keuka Lake facility. Shown is his successful Model E flying boat. (A flying boat is a seaplane that floats directly on its fuselage, the central part of the plane; other seaplanes—floatplanes—are kept afloat on pontoons.) Curtiss founded the Curtiss Aircraft Company, builders of illustrious military and civilian aircraft.

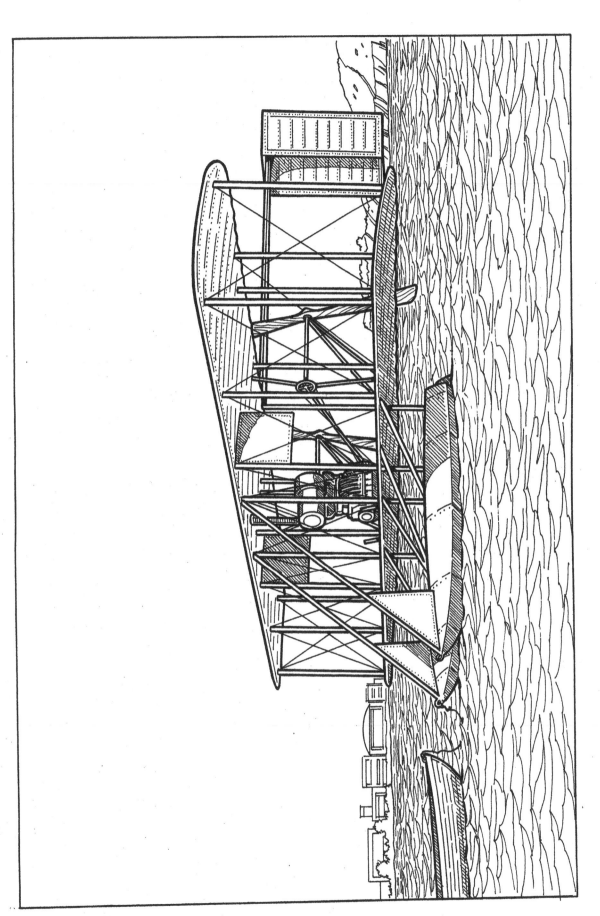

26. Wright Brothers Model B1 *Flyer*, 1912. In 1909, the U.S. Army Signal Corps purchased the Model A *Flyer*, which followed the *Flyer III*, to explore the military application of airplanes. In 1912, the U.S. Navy procured a Model B1 *Flyer* that was modified with a pontoon floats for water take-off and landing (shown here). This seaplane, along with the Glenn Curtiss Model E flying boat, formed the basis for the Navy's widely operated fleet of seaborne airplanes, which lasted well into the 1950s. The Wright Company also built a model G (1913–14), its only flying boat, as well as the CH (1913), a hydroplane on a single pontoon, and the K (1915), a seaplane.

27. Orville Wright and Charles Lindbergh, 1927. Depicted here is a 1927 meeting between Orville Wright and Charles Lindbergh, another great name in aviation history. Lindbergh had recently completed his epic solo flight across the Atlantic Ocean. He flew for 33 hours nonstop from New York to Paris in his Ryan monoplane, the *Spirit of St. Louis.* Lindbergh made several fruitless attempts to persuade Orville to write a firsthand account of the invention of the airplane, noting in his diary in 1939 that "Orville Wright is not an easy man to deal with in the matter." Fred Kelly's Wright brothers biography, "authorized by Orville Wright," appeared in 1942.

28. Orville Wright, 1947. Orville Wright is depicted here at age 77, shortly before his death in 1948. The contribution of Wilbur and Orville Wright to the technical, economic, and cultural progress of the 20th century cannot be overstated. The brothers took the idea of flight from imagination to reality, and in doing so, forever changed the world. Bishop Milton Wright's obituary for Wilbur summarizes the efforts of both of his sons, who achieved their goals by "seeing the right clearly" and "pursuing it steadily."